US WOMEN
WIN THE
WORLD CUP

by Brian Trusdell

SportsZone

An Imprint of Abdo Publishing
www.abdopublishing.com

Greatest Events in
SPORTS HISTORY

www.abdopublishing.com

Published by Abdo Publishing, a division of ABDO, PO Box 398166, Minneapolis, Minnesota 55439. Copyright © 2015 by Abdo Consulting Group, Inc. International copyrights reserved in all countries. No part of this book may be reproduced in any form without written permission from the publisher. SportsZone™ is a trademark and logo of Abdo Publishing.

Printed in the United States of America, North Mankato, Minnesota
092014
012015

Cover Photo: Lacy Atkins/The San Francisco Examiner/AP Images
Interior Photos: Lacy Atkins/The San Francisco Examiner/AP Images, 1; Duomo/Corbis, 4; Diether Endlicher/AP Images, 7; Press Association/AP Images, 9; Gilbert Iundt/TempSport/Corbis, 10; Ron Frehm/AP Images, 15; Philippe Caron/Sygma/Corbis, 16; Paul Sakuma/AP Images, 21; Bill Kostroun/AP Images, 22; George Tiedemann/Corbis, 24; Greg Gibson/AP Images, 26; John Todd/isiphotos.com/Corbis, 29; Nick Ut/AP Images, 30; Mark J. Terrill/AP Images, 33, 37; Eric Risberg/AP Images, 34; Michael Caulfield/AP Images, 39; Marcio Jose Sanchez/AP Images, 43

Editor: Chrös McDougall
Series Designer: Craig Hinton

Library of Congress Control Number: 2014944248

Cataloging-in-Publication Data
Trusdell, Brian.
US women win the World Cup / Brian Trusdell.
    p. cm. -- (Greatest events in sports history)
ISBN 978-1-62403-599-9 (lib. bdg.)
Includes bibliographical references and index.
1. Soccer--United States--History--Juvenile literature. 2. Soccer players--United States--Juvenile literature. 3. Women soccer players--United States--Juvenile literature. 4. World Cup (Soccer)--Juvenile literature.   I. Title.
796.334--dc23

2014944248

CONTENTS

ONE
Getting Noticed • 5

TWO
Making the Team • 11

THREE
Creating an Event• 17

FOUR
Big from the Start• 23

FIVE
The Final • 31

SIX
The Legacy • 39

Timeline	44
Glossary	45
For More Information	46
Index	48
About the Author	48

US star Mia Hamm controls the ball during the 1996 Olympic Games.

CHAPTER 1

Getting Noticed

The US women's soccer team went to the first Women's World Cup in 1991 and won. Yet in 1995, the team's average home crowd was just 4,392. Some high school football games draw more people than that. The players were used to playing outside of the spotlight. Then, in 1996, that changed.

The 1996 Olympic Games were held in Atlanta, Georgia. Women's soccer was an Olympic sport for the first time. And on August 1 of that year, 76,481 fans packed Sanford Stadium at the University of Georgia in Athens. It was the sport's first gold-medal game. The crowd helped cheer the US women to a 2–1 victory over China.

IN THE News

The sellout crowd at the 1996 Olympic gold-medal game stunned US reporters. Before the Olympics, the US women had never played before a home crowd larger than 8,975. A *USA Today* reporter described the scene.

> They came through the turnstiles, repeating the request over and over.
>
> "Please don't rip it."
>
> Don't worry, the ticket-taker said, carefully tearing off the end but leaving the rest of the prized possession intact. For the fans who filled more than 70,000 seats Thursday at Sanford Stadium—the largest crowd to see a women's sports event in the world—this was more than a ticket into the first Olympic women's soccer final between the USA and China.
>
> It was a souvenir.

Source: Mark Woods. "USA-China Spectators Treasure Ticket to History." USA Today, *August 2, 1996. Print. 6E.*

It was a special moment for women's soccer. And the attention continued to the next day. The US women arrived at the main press center. A pack of reporters was on hand to ask questions. Photographers and TV cameras captured the moment. It had been a long 12 hours for the players. But they came onto the stage smiling. They wore their gold medals around their necks.

US goalie Briana Scurry, *left*, and forward Carin Gabarra carry an American flag after the team beat China to win the 1996 Olympic gold medal.

Midfielder Julie Foudy was 25 years old. She had been playing with the national team for eight years. During that time she had played in front of countless small crowds. Yet she had also won a World Cup and now an Olympic gold medal. She didn't have much else to prove in soccer. Some wondered if Foudy and some of her teammates might retire from playing. After all, there was no established women's professional league for club teams. Plus, most of the players had college degrees. They could leave the sport to find a better-paying career. But they wanted more.

The 1994 men's World Cup had been held in the United States. It had been a huge success. The 1996 Olympics then brought new

OLYMPIC WOMEN'S SOCCER

Men's soccer made its Olympic debut in 1900 and has been in every event since 1920. Women's soccer had to wait until 1996. Eight teams were divided into two, four-team groups. The first-round games were played as part of doubleheaders with men's games. Both women's semifinals were held as a doubleheader. The bronze-medal and gold-medal games were held back-to-back as well. The Olympic men's soccer tournament is for players 23 years old and younger. However, there is no age limit in the women's tournament.

attention to women's soccer. But Foudy and her teammates wanted to see the women's game grow even bigger.

"Our goal is to try to reach a bigger audience," Foudy said at the press conference. "It's a step-by-step progression. Some are baby steps. Others are like last night."

The players knew their next opportunity for a big step. Fédération Internationale de Football Association (FIFA) governs soccer around the world. Two months before the Olympics, FIFA named the United States the host of the 1999 Women's World Cup.

Getting there would take sacrifice, though. Most of the US women on the team were in their mid-20s. They needed to train every day but also somehow make a living. At the time, the highest level they could play in the United States was the W-League. The low pay meant it was semipro at best. Some of the players were paid only a small amount of money to cover their expenses.

US soccer fans celebrate at the 1996 Olympic women's soccer tournament.

The 1996 Olympics had been encouraging. Three of the five US games attracted more than 55,000 fans. But players were also discouraged at times. None of their games had been played in Atlanta. Also, the NBC television network didn't show the championship game.

"Absolutely it was a lost opportunity," US coach Tony DiCicco said. "Americans have a love affair with the Olympics. And all those fans of [sports] that don't know soccer missed a chance to see it."

Soccer wouldn't have to compete with other sports at the Women's World Cup. So the players and US officials set out to give fans a memorable show.

CHAPTER 2

Michelle Akers celebrates after leading the United States to victory at the 1991 Women's World Cup.

Making the Team

Men's soccer had been long established by 1996. Women's soccer was still just beginning. For decades, women had been discouraged from playing soccer. In some countries, women were not even allowed to play. Those attitudes and rules finally began to change in the 1970s.

The United States became a leader in women's sports in 1972. A federal law that year called Title IX barred gender discrimination in high school and college sports. That meant schools and colleges that offered men's sports also had to offer women's sports. Women's soccer benefitted greatly. By the 1980s, many colleges had well-established programs. Those teams produced great players. And those players made up the US national team, which was founded in 1985.

The United States won the first Women's World Cup in 1991. Four years later the Americans finished third. Success did not necessarily result in popularity, though. Few people had heard of the Women's World Cup at the time. The 1996 Olympics had raised the sport's profile. There was still a long way to go, though.

One way to gain popularity was to keep winning. And there was no better place to win than on home soil at the 1999 Women's World Cup. Coach Tony DiCicco was tasked with leading the team there. The journey began when he called the squad together in January 1997.

DiCicco knew he would have to make some changes. The biggest was with forward Michelle Akers. Akers had been playing for the US team since 1985, when she was 19. She was the team's leading scorer with 92 goals in 109 games. But a new generation of players was taking over. Forwards Mia Hamm and Tiffeny Milbrett were world-class scorers. The team also had talented attacking midfielders in Julie Foudy and Kristine Lilly. So DiCicco asked Akers to switch positions. As holding midfielder, she could be an anchor for the attacking players. The move helped extend Akers's career. It also cleared the way for the 25-year-old Hamm to become the

MIA HAMM

Mariel Margaret "Mia" Hamm was becoming the face of US women's soccer. She had made her first national team appearance as a 15-year-old in 1987. Nobody younger had played for the US team through 2014. Hamm developed into a lethal scorer during the 1990s. She was ruthless on the field. Yet off the field, she was well-spoken and approachable. Sportswriters and fans alike were drawn to her. A famous 1999 Gatorade commercial featured Hamm and basketball superstar Michael Jordan. They competed against each other in a variety of sports. There was even a Mia Hamm Barbie doll before the 1999 Women's World Cup. Though she said she was uncomfortable with the attention, Hamm did her best to embrace it. She knew she was an important ambassador for the growing sport.

star. Already she had scored 63 goals in 120 games. Only Akers had more.

Defenders Carla Overbeck and Joy Fawcett had also joined the team in the late 1980s. More key players joined in the early- to mid-1990s. Among them were Shannon MacMillan, Cindy Parlow, and Brandi Chastain. That group gave DiCicco a strong foundation. All were talented players with experience playing together.

The US women played 18 games in 1997 and won 16. Among those wins were 12 in a row. And many of the wins were lopsided. The United States beat South Korea 7–0 and 6–1. Then the team beat England 5–0 and 6-0. Australia, meanwhile, fell 9–1 to the United States. Hamm scored 18 goals that year to lead the team.

IN THE News

The US women beat Portugal 7–0 on January 27, 1999, in Orlando, Florida. But, as *USA Today* reported, coach Tony DiCicco and his players weren't satisfied.

So why does DiCicco sound cautious before preparing to meet Portugal again Saturday in Fort Lauderdale, Florida? "We're still in the testing mode," he says. *"We have a lot of things to work on."*

His restless, perfection-driven players feel the same way. "It's our nature," team captain Carla Overbeck says. "We watched the game on film, and there were some things we did not do well."

Source: Peter Brewington. "DiCicco, Women's Players Have Set a High Standard." USA Today, *January 29, 1999. Print. 13C.*

The next year was even better. The US women won 22 games, tied two, and lost one. Hamm again led the team with 20 goals. She became only the third woman to score 100 goals for her country.

The 1999 Women's World Cup kicked off in June. On January 4, the US players began a full-time training camp in Sanford, Florida. The players signed contracts that paid for their housing. They also received a monthly salary from the US Soccer Federation (USSF).

US forward Mia Hamm (9) battles with Liu Ailing of China during a 1998 game in Uniondale, New York.

The team practiced every day. Sometimes they practiced twice a day. The year started with 7–0 and 6–0 wins over Portugal. Then they had 9–0 and 7–0 victories over Japan. But the results were different against stronger teams such as China. The United States played China three times in March and April. The Americans won only one game and lost the other two. The US women ended on a high note, though. They won their last seven games before the start of the World Cup. They outscored their opponents 35–2 in that time. Since the 1996 Olympics, the Americans had won 53 games, tied three, and lost just five. They clearly were one of the best teams in the world. But were they the best?

CHAPTER 3

Creating an Event

Marla Messing was never a soccer fan growing up. She never played the game. She never watched the game. Yet she played a major role in growing soccer in the United States.

Messing was a corporate lawyer at a law firm called Latham & Watkins. USSF president Alan Rothenberg was a partner there. And when Rothenberg needed help running the 1994 men's World Cup, he asked Messing. She became vice president in charge of special events and ticketing. Under her watch, the World Cup sold approximately 3.6 million tickets. That was still a record in 2014. After the World Cup, Messing helped launch Major League Soccer (MLS). She left the league when it began in the spring of 1996. Messing was 32 years old. She was ready to start a family.

WINNING OVER FANS

In 1998, a *Sports Illustrated* article declared, "There's no debating the gender of America's most avid soccer fans. They're girls." MLS was still a very young league at the time. Broadcasts of European men's games were rare in the United States. Yet 5.7 million US girls played the sport in 1998. Professional athletes are often detached from their fans. The US women's soccer team took the opposite approach. The players tried to connect with their young fans through constant appearances, clinics, and autograph sessions. It worked. In the lead-up to the 1999 Women's World Cup, young fans—nicknamed "pigtailed hooligans"—were known to mob the US players for autographs. One young fan explained why she was a fan of the US team. "I'd rather see girls play," she said. "I can relate to the girls. We can aspire to be like them."

Rothenberg soon came calling again, though. On May 31, 1996, FIFA announced that the United States would host the 1999 Women's World Cup. Rothenberg had big plans for the event. He wanted big stadiums, big crowds, and the media coverage to match. That was a bold goal. The 1995 Women's World Cup had been held in Sweden. Game crowds were as small as 655. The average was just 4,316 per game. But Rothenberg saw the crowds of 76,000 at the 1996 Olympics. He had visions of doing that again in 1999. So he called on Messing to achieve his vision. She was pregnant at the time. But she saw his offer as a challenge and accepted.

Not everybody shared their vision. FIFA worried that Rothenberg and Messing were thinking too big. Officials feared that the 1999 tournament would lose millions of dollars. Even some within the USSF had their doubts. But by November 19, 1997, there was no turning back. The organizers announced their plan.

The tournament's 32 games would be played in eight stadiums. The locations stretched from one side of the United States to the other. Seven stadiums were used regularly for pro or major college football. The biggest of those was the Rose Bowl in Pasadena, California. It seated more than 92,000 fans. The 1994 World Cup final had also been held there.

The organizers also favored doubleheaders. That meant two games in one day at the stadium. Only the two semifinal games were held on their own. This approach helped reduce the costs of renting the stadium. In addition, organizers hoped having four teams each day would draw more fans.

Ticket sales started slow, however. With a year to go, the organizers had sold 130,000 tickets. That was only 20 percent of the total tickets available. So Messing and her team stepped up their marketing. They used the phrase: "This is my game. This is my

IN THE News

Organizers had huge expectations for the 1999 Women's World Cup. However, a *New York Times* story from May 1999 considered the potential for disaster.

> Should the American women not reach the final, the World Cup is not very likely to transcend the base of suburban interest—the grass-roots soccer community, soccer dads and moms, and their teenage and preteen girls—to which the event is being primarily marketed. An unlikely early exit by the United States could result in largely empty stadiums and vacant interest by the American public. But, through clever packaging requirements, organizers have sold an average of 14,000 tickets for non–United States games in the first round.

Source: Jere Longman. "SOCCER; 1999 Women's World Cup: Beautiful Game Takes Flight." *The New York Times.* The New York Times Company, *May 20, 1985.* Web. Accessed June 20, 2014.

future. Watch me play." The hope was to attract the many young soccer-playing girls.

Ticket sales started to pick up in February 1999. That spring, the US women played a series of final friendly games called "The Road to the World Cup." More than 27,000 went to see a 3–0 victory over Mexico at the Rose Bowl. Nearly 24,000 watched a 2–1 loss to

Marla Messing, *above*, and Alan Rothenberg set out to make the 1999 Women's World Cup a major event.

China at Giants Stadium in New Jersey. More than 25,000 attended a game in Chicago's Soldier Field. The US team won that game 3–0 over the Netherlands.

"It was that whole Road to the World Cup," Messing said. "We started to see people wearing Women's World Cup T-shirts. People were really excited, the crowds were building."

Interest was building. But it was interest in the US women's team. Messing needed the US women's team to do well for the tournament to succeed. It was the one thing she couldn't control.

The United States plays Denmark in the opening game of the 1999 Women's World Cup. A sellout crowd attended the game at Giants Stadium in New Jersey.

CHAPTER 4

Big from the Start

The New Jersey Turnpike was jammed as cars squeezed to get off at exit 16W. Other roads leading to Giants Stadium also were bumper-to-bumper. The gates for the Women's World Cup opened on June 19. The United States was set to play Denmark in the opener. A crowd of 78,972 was ready. Giants Stadium had hosted seven games during the 1994 World Cup. None of those games had so many fans. And no women's sporting event had ever been played in front of such a large crowd.

It took only 17 minutes for the Americans to take the lead. Brandi Chastain sent a long diagonal ball to Mia Hamm on the right side. Hamm cut inside and unleashed a shot. The ball went just under the crossbar into the top of the net. The crowd

Brandi Chastain, *right*, celebrates with Julie Foudy after Foudy scored against Denmark in the 1999 World Cup opener.

erupted with chants of "U-S-A! U-S-A!" Americans Julie Foudy and Kristine Lilly added goals for a 3–0 win.

The United States played Nigeria five days later. Another packed house of 65,080 filled Chicago's Soldier Field. The start wasn't as positive as the last game, though. Less than two minutes into the game, Foudy headed the ball back in front of the US goal. But Nigeria's Nkiru Okosieme chipped it past US goalkeeper Briana Scurry.

NOT JUST THE GIRLS

Tournament organizers hoped young soccer-playing girls would fill the stadiums. And they did. But they were hardly the only ones. Many men and young boys also attended the matches. David Letterman became one of the team's biggest fans. The late-night talk show host promoted the team throughout the tournament. Mia Hamm and Brandi Chastain later appeared on his show after the tournament. Observers credited the tournament's mainstream appeal with boosting the credibility of female athletes.

It took 20 minutes for the United States to recover. The comeback began when a Nigerian defender scored an own goal. She tipped a free kick by Hamm past her own keeper. Less than a minute later, Hamm scored. Then Tiffeny Milbrett added a goal three minutes after that. By halftime, the United States was ahead 6–1. Milbrett added another goal for a 7–1 final score.

The United States still had to play North Korea in its third group-stage game. A berth in the knockout round was virtually assured for the Americans, though. So coach Tony DiCicco rested some of his regulars against North Korea. A crowd of 50,484 still showed up to watch in Foxborough, Massachusetts.

Michelle Akers, Foudy, Milbrett, and Kate Sobrero did not start. Tiffany Roberts, Sara Whalen, Shannon MacMillan, and Tisha Venturini took their places. MacMillan put the Americans ahead in the 56th minute. Venturini added two more goals in a 3–0 victory.

President Bill Clinton and his family pose with the US players after their quarterfinal win over Germany.

The win put the United States atop Group A. That set up a quarterfinal match against Germany. Attendance at the stadiums had already been huge. Interest was growing nationally, too. The United States-Germany quarterfinal was held in Landover, Maryland. Demand for tickets was so big that officials opened the upper deck of the stadium. On game day, 54,642 fans filed into Jack Kent Cooke Stadium.

The game again got off to a bad start. Chastain tried to pass back to Scurry in the fifth minute. Instead, the ball went into the net for an own goal. Milbrett tied the game 11 minutes later. But Bettina Wiegmann restored the lead for Germany just before halftime.

Chastain made up for her earlier mistake in the 49th minute. She volleyed a corner kick into the goal. The United States secured the win in the 65th minute. MacMillan took a corner kick. Joy Fawcett headed it into goal for a 3–2 win.

World Cup organizers had high hopes for the tournament. They hoped to attract the attention of the young girls who were soccer players. Those girls indeed took notice. But so did a lot of other people—including boys and men. Even President Bill Clinton and his family attended the Germany game. President Clinton congratulated the US players afterward. But they had little time to celebrate. They were off to Stanford, California. A semifinal against Brazil was coming three days later on July 4.

Another enthusiastic crowd arrived dressed in red, white, and blue. The 73,123 fans celebrated Independence Day with another US win. Cindy Parlow scored on a header in the fifth minute. Brazil put up a fight. But Scurry made several big saves. Then Akers ended

IN THE News

Many sportswriters ignored women's sports in the 1990s. They didn't believe the Women's World Cup would be worth paying attention to. Attitudes changed as the World Cup progressed, though. One *Washington Post* writer compared the US win over Brazil to some of sport's all-time greats.

Today's US soccer victory and the spectacle of pride and patriotism fell on a date remembered for other momentous occasions in American sports: the triumph of the first black heavyweight boxing champion, Jack Johnson over Jim Jeffries in the "Fight of the Century" on July 4, 1910, and one of the saddest days in the nation's sports history, July 4, 1939, when terminally ill Lou Gehrig bade farewell to a nation at Yankee Stadium.

The US soccer team hopes to be long remembered as an inspiring force in women's sports, and needs one more victory to claim the Women's World Cup.

Source: William Gildea. "U.S. Women March Into Soccer Final; At Wimbledon It's an American Sweep." Washington Post, July 5, 1999. Print. A01.

any doubt in the 80th minute. She scored on a penalty kick to secure a 2–0 victory.

Tournament organizers had bet on the US team doing well in the tournament. The Americans had certainly done their part so

The US players line up for the national anthem before the semifinal game against Brazil in Stanford, California.

far. Now they were on to the final. Meanwhile, China easily beat

Norway 5–0 in the other semifinal. That set up a rematch of the

1996 Olympic gold-medal game.

US star Mia Hamm answers questions from reporters two days before the 1999 Women's World Cup final.

CHAPTER 5

The Final

Many people had doubted that a women's soccer tournament could be a major event. But for three weeks, the Women's World Cup had been hugely popular. More and more people tuned in to each game. The media couldn't get enough of the star US player, Mia Hamm. By the time the final was played on July 10, the Women's World Cup was the biggest sports story in the country.

The United States and China took the field on a picturesque Saturday afternoon in Pasadena, California. The temperature had climbed to 90 degrees Fahrenheit (32°C) by the 1:00 p.m. kickoff. A crowd of 90,185 filled the Rose Bowl. An estimated 40 million Americans tuned in on TV. That kind of audience was unheard of for a women's sporting event. Among those in attendance was President Bill Clinton. Like many Americans, he had become a fan.

The sold-out stadium guaranteed that the tournament would make a profit. Now all the United States had to do was win. But that was no easy task. China had beaten the US team twice in three games earlier in the year.

Both teams could score goals. They were the tournament's two top-scoring teams. So defense was the priority on both sides. The United States put its attention on forward Sun Wen. Her seven goals were tied for the tournament lead. China had to stop a more balanced US attack. Tiffeny Milbrett led all US players with three goals. Five other players had two goals.

Both teams were successful in their defensive lockdowns. The game was a tight, tense affair. Neither team scored in the first 45 minutes. The game remained scoreless after 90 minutes, as well. But the United States lost a key player just before the whistle. Michelle Akers collided with goalkeeper Briana Scurry on a corner kick. Akers slumped to the turf with a concussion. She was taken to the locker room and treated for dehydration. Regulation time ended with the score still tied 0–0.

China's Zhang Ouying (7) tries to dribble past US defender Joy Fawcett (14) during the 1999 Women's World Cup final.

Sara Whalen replaced Akers as the game went into extra time. The first team to score would win the game. China came close in the 100th minute. Liu Ying curled a corner kick from the left side. Teammate Fan Yunjie headed it toward goal. Scurry was out of position. The crowd gasped. But Christine Lilly was guarding the near post and headed the ball off the line. After 120 minutes, the score was still 0–0.

US goalie Briana Scurry blocks Liu Ying's shot during the shootout in the 1999 World Cup final.

Now the championship would come down to a shootout. Each team would get five penalty kicks. China would shoot first. Whichever team scored more would win.

The US coaches had to decide on five players to take the penalties. Assistant Lauren Gregg made a list. Coach Tony DiCicco noticed the list did not include Brandi Chastain. She had missed two penalties already that year. One of the misses had come in a 2–1 loss to China. But DiCicco had a hunch. He asked Chastain if she could make her penalty. The confident woman, whom teammates called "Hollywood," quickly said yes.

The first two shooters from each team scored. Liu came up third for China. She was the only Chinese player so far who had played

BRANDI CHASTAIN

Brandi Chastain's reaction to her winning penalty kick became a symbol for the US victory. The picture was shown everywhere. It even landed on the covers of magazines such as *Sports Illustrated* and *Newsweek*. Fans who had not known much about women's soccer knew Chastain. She later wrote an autobiography. In 2000, Nike featured her in a TV commercial with basketball star Kevin Garnett. A museum even displayed her famous sports bra for a time. It was an amazing rise in fame for a player who wasn't even in the original shootout lineup.

the entire game. As Liu shot, Scurry lunged away from her line to her left with both hands. She was spot on. Scurry blocked the ball. She immediately jumped up, pumping her arms. The crowd, already on its feet, erupted. Kristine Lilly then continued the celebration. Her shot into the upper left corner of the net put the United States ahead 3–2.

China's Zhang Ouying and the United States' Mia Hamm both made their shots. That brought up Sun, China's best scorer. And she calmly blasted a low ball past Scurry. That brought up Chastain with a chance to win.

Standing two steps inside the penalty area, Chastain waited for the referee's whistle. She took four quick steps. Then she curled her left-footed shot toward the right post. China goalie Gao Hong dived toward the ball. She never came close. It hit the back of the net just inside the right post.

Newspapers splashed the story of the US win across their front pages. One of those front-page stories appeared in the *New York Times.*

Chastain's kick consummated three weeks of unprecedented interest in a sport that filled huge arenas with soccer moms and dads and their daughters, who painted their faces red, white and blue in a star-spangled admiration of the American players. Grownups finally began recognizing the sporting heroes their kids had discovered long ago. Even President Clinton was in attendance today, having been drawn into the swirl of popularity surrounding the United States team.

Source: Jere Longman. "Refusing to Wilt, US Wins Soccer Title." New York Times, July 11, 1999. Print. 1.

Chastain ripped off her jersey. She fell to her knees, fists clenched. Her teammates surrounded her while the crowd exploded in cheers. Three weeks earlier, most Americans had never heard of the US women's soccer team. Now, the players were world champions and national heroes.

The images of the confident, athletic Brandi Chastain celebrating World Cup victory in her sports bra became iconic.

Carla Overbeck, *with trophy*, and her US teammates celebrate after winning the 1999 Women's World Cup.

CHAPTER 6

The Legacy

Even before the last piece of confetti fell at the Rose Bowl, the Women's World Cup was declared a success. Never before had a women's sporting event received so much mainstream attention. Media covered the World Cup as a major event. Fan interest grew throughout the tournament. It certainly didn't hurt that the US players embraced the attention—and won.

The tournament ended up drawing 1,194,221 fans to 32 games. The average attendance was 37,319. That was far beyond expectations. In the United States, 17.9 million viewers watched the final on ABC. That remained a record for a US soccer broadcast until the 2014 men's World Cup. FIFA organizers had worried about the tournament losing money. Instead, the Women's World Cup made approximately $2 million.

After the tournament, many US players became known as "The '99ers." Many were household names. Major companies signed them to endorsement contracts. Mia Hamm was the face of the team. But Brandi Chastain provided the lasting image of the tournament.

Soccer boosters saw the 1999 World Cup as a turning point for women's sports. Title IX had been in effect for more than 25 years. Generations of US girls had grown up playing sports. Some of those girls developed into world-class athletes. Now, for the first time, women's team sports had a high-profile championship. The World Cup had shown what was possible. The next step would be to build on that popularity.

That proved harder than expected. Much had gone right at the 1999 World Cup. It occurred at a time of rising interest and participation in women's sports in the United States. Fans were drawn to the charismatic US players. Plus, the US team won the tournament in exciting fashion. As USSF General Secretary Hank Steinbrecher liked to say, organizers "caught lightning in a bottle."

GOING PRO

The 1999 Women's World Cup had been a huge success. The next step seemed to be a professional women's league in the United States. Attempts to create one have struggled, though. The Women's United Soccer Association (WUSA) began in 2002. Several stars from the 1999 US team played in the league. But the WUSA struggled to live up to its own lofty expectations. Team owners lost millions of dollars. In 2003, they decided to fold the WUSA. Another league launched in 2009 but suffered a similar fate. Fans hope that the National Women's Soccer League can change that. It launched in 2013. The US, Canadian, and Mexican soccer federations help fund the league. That gives it more stability than the previous leagues. Many of the best players from those countries play in the league.

Comparisons to 1999 have continued to follow women's soccer. No event has since matched the tournament's popularity. The sport has seen tremendous growth, though. Attendance at the 2003 World Cup was nearly 680,000 for 32 games. That was modest compared to 1999. However, it was nearly five times higher than the attendance at the 1995 World Cup.

Meanwhile, interest and development has grown around the world. In the early years of the sport, the United States, China, Germany, and Norway dominated. Since 1999, Brazil, Canada, France, Japan, and Sweden are also contenders. Many other countries have grown competitive. That led FIFA to include 24 teams in the 2015 Women's World Cup. The previous four events only had 16 teams.

IN THE News

The 2011 Women's World Cup showed that women's soccer was indeed growing. A *Sports Illustrated* article noted how popular the event had become around the world.

If the '99 Women's World Cup was the ultimate vindication of Title IX in the US, this year's tournament is exporting Title IX on a global level. German fans have followed the games in record numbers, with more than 73,000 supporters filling Olympic Stadium in Berlin for the home side's opening victory against Canada, and nearly 700,000 tickets sold for the Cup's 32 games. Even more striking have been the television ratings, which set records for women's soccer in Canada and Germany.

Source: Grant Wahl. "Global Warming." Sports Illustrated. *Time Inc.*, July 18, 2011. Web. Accessed July 18, 2014.

Fans continue to compare the US team to the '99ers as well. The United States won an Olympic gold medal in 2004. Few '99ers remained with the team after that. In their places, new stars such as forward Abby Wambach and goalie Hope Solo emerged. The United States won Olympic gold medals in 2008 and 2012. But it was the 2011 World Cup where they again truly captured the country's attention. The ESPN networks aired all 32 games

A new generation of US stars such as Abby Wambach has continued to build upon the foundation set by the 1999 US women's national team.

from Germany. US fans followed as the American team made a dramatic run to the final. Although the United States lost to Japan, approximately 13.5 million US fans watched on TV. At the time, only five English-language soccer broadcasts had ever drawn more fans in the United States. At the top of that list, however, was the 1999 Women's World Cup final.

TIMELINE

August 18, 1985

The US women's national soccer team plays its first game. It loses 1–0 to Italy in Jesolo, Italy.

1991

The United States wins the first Women's World Cup (then called the Women's World Championship).

May 31, 1996

FIFA awards the 1999 Women's World Cup to the United States.

August 1, 1996

A crowd of 76,489—a record for a women's sporting event—watches the United States beat China 2–1 in the Olympic gold-medal game.

November 19, 1997

The Women's World Cup organizing committee announces its plans to host the Women's World Cup in big stadiums.

January 4, 1999

The US women's national team convenes for a full-time training camp in Sanford, Florida.

June 19, 1999

A crowd of 78,972 fills Giants Stadium in New Jersey to watch the Women's World Cup openers. The US team beats Denmark 3–0, and Brazil beats Mexico 7–1.

July 1, 1999

The United States twice rallies from a goal down to beat Germany 3–2 in the quarterfinals in front of a crowd of 54,642 in Maryland.

July 10, 1999

The United States outlasts China 5–4 in a shootout to win the Women's World Cup. The crowd of 90,185 fans at the Rose Bowl in Pasadena, California, and the 17.9 million US TV viewers are records for women's sporting events.

2011

The US women's national team steps out of the shadow of the '99ers during a dramatic run to the Women's World Cup final. Approximately 13.5 million US fans watch the final on TV.

club team

A team that a player plays for throughout the year. National teams draw players from club teams.

concussion

A brain injury caused by a blow to the head.

contracts

Legal agreements between two parties, such as a player and a team.

doubleheaders

Sporting events in which two games are played back to back in the same stadium.

endorsement

To promote a company or its products, often for pay.

extra time

Soccer's version of overtime. If a game is tied after 90 minutes, and a winner must be determined, two more periods of 15 minutes are played.

friendly

An exhibition soccer game that is not part of a league or tournament.

group stage

In the Women's World Cup, this is the first round. Four teams play each other once, and the top two teams advance to the knockout round.

knockout round

The second round of the Women's World Cup. The best teams from the group stage meet in a single elimination bracket to determine the champion.

national team

An all-star team that is made up of a country's best players. All of the players on the team are citizens of the country they represent.

own goal

A term used when a player accidentally puts the ball into his or her own net, scoring a goal for the opponent.

shootout

If the game is still tied after extra time, a penalty kick shootout is used to decide the winner. Five players from each team take a penalty shot.

volley

A kick to an airborne ball.

FOR MORE INFORMATION

SELECTED BIBLIOGRAPHY

Allaway, Roger, Colin Jose, and David Litterer. *The Encyclopedia of American Soccer History.* Lanham, MD: Scarecrow, 2001. Print.

Bondy, Filip. "Victory Sweet for US Women, Beat China in Tie-Break Shootout as Games Ends in Deadlock." *New York Daily News,* July 11, 1999. Print. 5.

Jensen, Mike. "US Women's Team on Top of the World: Outlasts China 5–4 on Penalty Kicks After Playing to a Goalless Draw." *The Gazette (Montreal),* July 12, 1999. Print. B1.

Mihoces, Gary. "USA's Win Turns Groans into Cheers, 'First Family' among 54,642 Attending Quarterfinal Game." *USA Today.* July 2, 1999. Print. 11C.

US Soccer Communications Department. *2013 US Women's National Team Media Guide.* Peoria, IL: US Soccer Communications Department, 2013. Print.

FURTHER READINGS

Chastain, Brandi. *It's Not About the Bra: Play Hard, Play Fair, and Put the Fun Back Into Competitive Sports.* New York: William Morrow, 2004. Print.

Christopher, Matt. *In the Goal With . . . Briana Scurry.* New York: Little, Brown, 2000. Print.

Coffey, Wayne. *An Inside Look at America's Teams (Meet The Women of American Soccer).* New York: Scholastic, 1999. Print.

Hamm, Mia, and Aaron Heifetz. *Go For the Goal: A Champion's Guide to Winning in Soccer and Life.* New York: It Books, 2000. Print.

Longman, Jere. *The Girls of Summer: The US Women's Soccer Team and How It Changed the World.* New York: Harper Collins, 2001. Print.

US Soccer Federation. *100 Years of Soccer in America.* New York: Universe, 2013. Print.

WEBSITES

To learn more about the Greatest Events in Sports History, visit **booklinks.abdopublishing.com**. These links are routinely monitored and updated to provide the most current information available.

PLACES TO VISIT

FedEx Field
1600 Fedex Way
Landover, MD 20785
(301) 276-6000
www.redskins.com/fedexfield
FedEx Field opened in August 1997 and is home to the National Football League's Washington Redskins. The stadium was originally called Jack Kent Cooke Stadium after the owner of the Redskins, who died April 6, 1997. The stadium was the site of the 1999 Women's World Cup quarterfinal game between the United States and Germany. The United States twice rallied from a one-goal deficit to win 3–2.

Rose Bowl
1001 Rose Bowl Dr.
Pasadena, CA 91103
(626) 577-3100
www.rosebowlstadium.com
The Rose Bowl is one of the largest stadiums in the United States, with a capacity of more than 90,000. It was opened in 1922. Besides being the site of the annual Rose Bowl college football game, it is the regular home for UCLA football games. It was the site of the 1999 Women's World Cup soccer final and the 1994 men's World Cup soccer final.

INDEX

Akers, Michelle, 12–13, 25, 28, 32–33

Australia, 13

Chastain, Brandi, 13, 23, 25, 27, 34–36, 40

China, 5, 6, 15, 21, 24, 31–35, 41

Clinton, Bill, 27, 32, 36

Denmark, 23

DiCicco, Tony, 9, 12–13, 14, 25, 34

England, 13

Fawcett, Joy, 13, 27

Fédération Internationale de Football Association (FIFA), 8, 18, 19, 39, 40

Foudy, Julie, 7–8, 12, 24–25

Garnett, Kevin, 35

Gregg, Lauren, 34

Hamm, Mia, 12–14, 23, 25, 31, 35, 40

Hong, Gao, 35

Jordan, Michael, 13

Letterman, David, 25

Lilly, Kristine, 12, 24, 33, 35

MacMillan, Shannon, 13, 25, 27

Major League Soccer (MLS), 17, 18

Messing, Marla, 17–19, 21

Mexico, 20, 41

Milbrett, Tiffeny, 12, 25, 27, 32

National Women's Soccer League (NWSL), 41

Nigeria, 24–25

Okosieme, Nkiru, 24

Olympic Games, 5, 6, 7–9, 12, 15, 18, 29, 42

Ouying, Zhang, 35

Overbeck, Carla, 13, 14

Parlow, Cindy, 13, 27

professional women's soccer, 7, 41

Roberts, Tiffany, 25

Rothenberg, Alan, 17–19

Scurry, Briana, 24, 27, 28, 32–33, 35

Sobrero, Kate, 25

Solo, Hope, 42

South Korea, 13

Title IX, 11, 40, 42

US Soccer Federation (USSF), 14, 17, 19

Venturini, Tisha, 25

Wambach, Abby, 42

Wen, Sun, 32, 35

Whalen, Sara, 25, 33

Wiegmann, Bettina, 27

Women's World Cup
1991, 5, 11, 12
1994, 7, 17, 19, 23
1995, 12
1999, 8, 14–15, 17–21, 23–29, 31–36, 39–43

World Cup (men's)
1994, 7, 17, 19, 23
2014, 39

Ying, Liu, 33, 34–35

Yunjie, Fan, 33

ABOUT THE AUTHOR

Brian Trusdell has covered soccer for more than 30 years, beginning in 1980 with the Pittsburgh Spirit in the MISL. He grew up as a fan of the Philadelphia Atoms in the NASL and has written about the sport for several outlets, including the Associated Press and Bloomberg News. He has covered four men's World Cups, two Women's World Cups, and six Olympic Games. Trusdell lives in New Jersey with his wife.